What Causes Weather and Seasons?

Alejandro Algarra / Rocío Bonilla

BARRON'S

"Kate, I wish it was warm out so we could go swimming," says Jack.

"Yeah, too bad it's not summer," adds Kate.

"Kate, why *are* there different seasons?" asks Jack. "And why is it so hot in the summer and so cold in the winter?"

"I was wondering the same thing!" replies Kate. "I want to know what makes weather change so much, and why trees lose their leaves in the fall."

"Let's look it up!" exclaims Jack.

The sun and the weather

The weather changes at different times of the year because of the sun. The sun is a huge ball of gas and fire at the center of our solar system. The sun's rays have been reaching Earth and giving us light and heat for billions of years.

The sun makes it possible for all types of weather to occur, such as clouds and rain, wind, and snow and ice. The sun heats up water on the ground and in lakes, rivers, and oceans. The water drops rise up into the air (called evaporation), where they cool down, stick together, and form clouds. When the clouds get really full of water, it rains! Or, if it's really cold outside, it snows! Pretty neat, right? This is called the water cycle.

5

The Earth spins

The Earth is a huge ball, or sphere, that spins around like a ballerina. At the same time as it's spinning, the Earth moves around the sun in a giant circle called an orbit. It takes 365 days (one year) to complete one orbit around the sun. Then it begins all over again! The Earth's movements make day and night, as well as the four seasons: spring, summer, fall, and winter.

Day and night, light and dark

It takes 24 hours, or one day, for Earth to make one complete spin, or rotation. That's why we have day and night! When the part of the Earth where you live faces the sun it is daytime, and when it faces away from the sun it is nighttime.

Usually, the sun heats us during the day and makes the air warmer.
At night, it is dark and the sun's heat is gone, so the air is colder.

Why are there seasons?

There is an imaginary line that wraps around the center of Earth like a belt. This line is called the Equator.

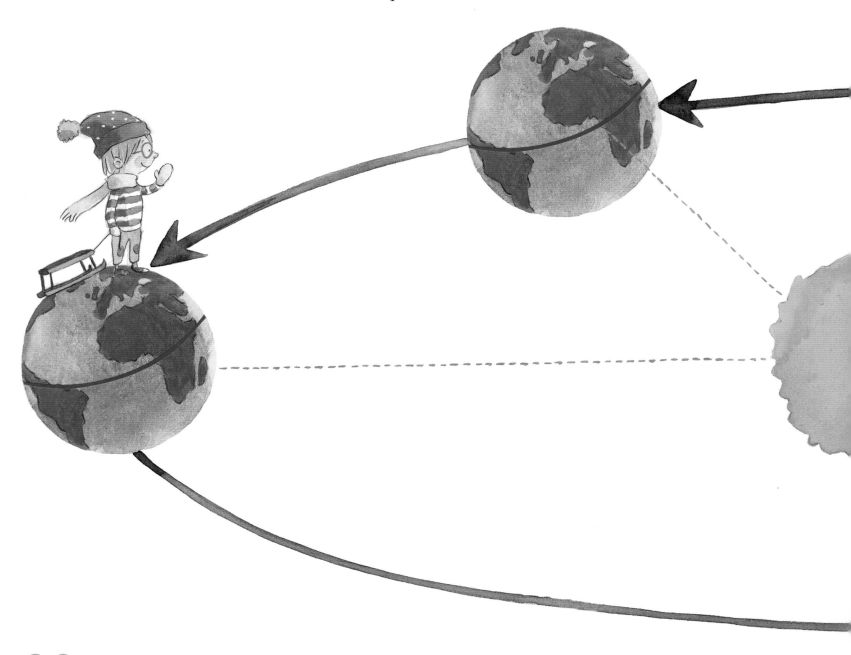

The Equator divides Earth into two parts: the north half and the south half, which are called hemispheres. As Earth orbits the sun, the heat and light from the sun reach the northern and southern hemispheres differently. This is why it is hot in some places while it is cold in others.

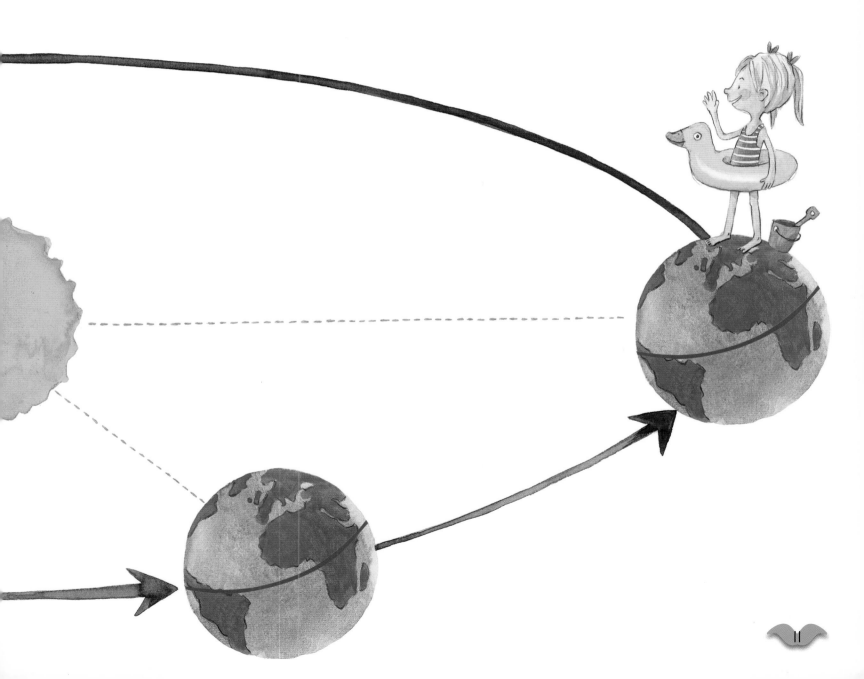

Springtime

Spring comes right after winter. There is more sunight now, so Earth heats up more during the day, and the weather starts to get warmer. But the spring can have many different types of weather! Some days it is really windy, while other days it rains or even hails. Some mornings are chilly, but it can become warm or even hot later in the day when the sun shines brightly.

14

Life blossoms in the spring

During this season, leaves and beautiful flowers grow on many plants and trees. Fruit trees fill with blossoms, which will become delicious fruit in just a few months! Most insects begin to come out, and animals mate so that their young will grow up in the summer when they'll have plenty of food to eat.

It's summer!

When spring is over, summer begins. The days are long and the nights are shorter, so the sun warms us for more hours. Many growing fruits and vegetables are ready to be eaten, and the sea water is also warmer. It's the best time to go swimming! In some places, however, the summer can be very hot and dry. This can cause what's called a drought—a long period of time when there is almost no rain. The lack of water during a drought can make it hard for people to grow food.

Summer storms

During the summer, huge storms are common. Summer storms can appear quickly and do not last long. The sky gets dark, lightning flashes from very tall clouds, thunder roars, and heavy rain falls for a few minutes. When it is over, the sky clears, and you may even see an amazing rainbow stretch across the sky!

Summer sun caution

Summer means vacation, sun, and beaches. But, beware! The sun is very strong in the summer, so it is important to protect your skin whenever you go outside.

If you are going to be outside all day, especially at the beach, make sure you use sunscreen! Also, it is better to try to stay in the shade during the middle of the day when the sun's rays are strongest.

The fall

In the northern hemisphere, fall begins in September and the weather changes again. The days are now shorter than the nights, so the sun doesn't warm things as much as it did in the spring and summer.
The weather starts to get chilly, and seas and lakes get cooler and cooler. You probably don't want to go swimming now!

Migratory birds and the grain harvest

Many birds migrate, or fly together toward the Equator, to spend the fall and winter in warmer areas. They assemble into huge groups in the sky and often make a V-shape as they fly. One example of a migratory bird is the swallow.

The fall is when grain and other crops are harvested, or picked. These include wheat, barley, pumpkins, and chestnuts.

Falling leaves

In the fall, nature gets ready for the cold winter weather. The leaves on many trees begin to change color, then turn brown, and later they fall off and the branches are left bare. This is how the trees protect themselves from the winter freeze. Insects have also been preparing for the weather change. They stored food underground during the summer so they can survive the cold weather when there is less food. When fall gives way to winter, insects will keep themselves sheltered from the cold, and their young will be born when the weather gets warm again.

Winter is here!

In December, winter arrives on the shortest day of the year. From this point on, there will be more sunlight with each passing day, but the days are still much shorter than the nights, so the weather gets even colder! The air and the ground are cold, and the chilly north wind blows. In some places, there are snowstorms, and ponds and lakes freeze. Fields and mountains are covered in a blanket of white. In the morning, the ground and trees are covered in ice. This is called frost. Brrrrr—it's so cold!

Ready for the cold

Life can be harder in the winter for some animals because it's not as easy to find food. Many animals, like groundhogs and some snakes, eat extra food in the summer and in the fall, and then they go to sleep during the winter in underground tunnels called burrows. This is called hibernation. Other animals, like squirrels, do not hibernate but they often stay in their dens to keep warm.

Kate and Jack are still cold from winter, but soon the weather will start to get warmer.

"Look, Jack! Do you see the bud sprouting on the tree?" says Kate. "Spring is almost here! Isn't that amazing?"

"Yes, it is!" replies Jack. "I found an ant coming out for food. . . looks like it's going to get warmer soon!"

Parent guide

In many parts of the northern hemisphere, we are used to a climate with four seasons. However, did you know that the seasons are different on the rest of the planet? When summer begins in the northern hemisphere, winter begins in the southern hemisphere. Then the opposite also happens: their summer is at the same time as our coldest months. And the other seasons, fall and spring, are also opposite to ours. Other places do not have such pronounced seasons as we do here. There are areas near the Equator where it is always hot and there is just a dry and a rainy season. There are also places where it almost never rains, such as deserts. Our seasons are:

SPRING

Spring begins on March 21 and ends on June 21. There can be rain, sun, and heavy winds all in the same day. In the countryside, the snow and ice that has accumulated in the mountains during the cold season begin to melt, and the water washes down the slopes, soaks into the ground, and fills the streams in the valleys.

Plant and animal life flourish in the spring. New leaves and flowers grow on trees and many shrubs and wild plants blossom. Animals that hibernate awaken from their sleep, insects are born from their eggs or emerge from their cocoons, and nature's activity begins to speed up. Migratory birds return to their summer homes, often to the same nest they left the previous year.

SUMMER

Summer begins on June 21 and ends September 21. In the northern hemisphere, it is the time when the Earth is the farthest from the sun (because the Earth's orbit around the sun is not circular but elliptical). The nights are short and the days are long, and some days are hot, sometimes even stifling. Some places may even suffer from droughts, especially where the winter and spring are drier. However, in other places where it rains in the summer, it usually rains hard! The typical summer storm comes with masses of very tall clouds (cumulonimbus), which unload huge downpours in just a few minutes. Afterward, the sky clears up quickly and not a trace of the storm remains.

Nature's activity reaches its peak in the summer: Mammals and birds care for their young that were born in the spring, and they prepare them for life. They teach them how to eat, hunt, hide, or flee, and birds help their young learn how to fly. Insects complete their life cycle. They fly among the flowers, eat, and reproduce. In the plant world, many spring flowers have turned into fruit, which ripen in the sun and are ready for their seeds to be spread by animals or the wind.

FALL

Fall begins on September 21 and ends on December 21. The weather varies, as it goes from being warm in early fall to cold by the end of the season. There is seasonal rain, which can be quite heavy at times. The wind is increasingly cold when it blows, and on the coast the sea water is cold and the waves fierce.

In nature, both plants and animals begin to prepare for the coldest season. Herbaceous plants disappear. They will spend the winter as seeds or bulbs nestled underground. Trees and shrubs begin to slow down. Their leaves die and turn from green to yellow, and later to brown, before they fall off. The animal world also gets ready for the cold weather. Some animals migrate to warmer climates. The best example is birds. They set off for warmer latitudes closer to the Equator. Other animals spend their days eating voraciously so they can accumulate enough energy reserves for the winter. Many animals, including mammals, reptiles, and amphibians dig out burrows or tunnels or take refuge, where they spend the winter sleeping. This process is called hibernation. Adult forms of various insects, with the exception of ants, bees, and many beetles, tend to die when the summer ends. They spend the winter buried as pupas or hardy eggs.

WINTER

Winter begins on December 21 and ends on March 21. It is the coldest season of the year. The sun lights up the Earth just a few hours a day, with rays that hit the Earth at a shallow angle. The temperatures drop sharply, especially at night. Instead of rain there is snow, and instead of dew there is frost. Ponds, streams, and other small bodies of water often freeze. In some places farther north, the surfaces of lakes freeze, even though the fish and plants on the bottom can easily survive in the water that remains under the ice. Life continues during this season, but it is dormant. Mammals like the brown bear, the dormouse, and the marmot hibernate until the spring. As for plants, those that can withstand the winter without losing their leaves predominate, such as coniferous plants. The needle shape of their leaves and the shape of their canopies allow them to easily bear heavy snowfalls.

First edition for the United States and Canada
published in 2016 by Barron's Educational
Series, Inc.

© Gemser Publications, S.L. 2015
El Castell, 38 08329 Teiá (Barcelona, Spain)
www.mercedesros.com

Text: Alejandro Algarra
Design and layout: Estudi Guasch, S.L.
Illustration: Rocio Bonilla

All inquiries should be addressed to:
Barron's Educational Series, Inc.
250 Wireless Boulevard
Hauppauge, NY 11788
www.barronseduc.com

ISBN: 978-1-4380-0892-9

Library of Congress Control No.: 2016930608

Date of Manufacture: April 2016
Manufactured by: L. Rex Printing Company
Limited, Dongguan City, Guangdong, China

Printed in China
9 8 7 6 5 4 3 2 1